Society

Author: Derrick Frohne

© 2010-Present Derrick Frohne
Publisher: Frohne

Acknowledgments

I want to thank my family, friends, and the people who read this book.

PREFACE

Ulterior unemployment in the United States continuously rises at an alarming rate. Even President Barack Obama admits that the country needs continuous assistance. He said that he stimulated the economy by providing bail out money to the banks and within two years and spent more than one trillion because of the recent recession. I am not alone when I say the vicissitudes the United States of America exemplifies a new great depression. Something must be done because American fanatics produce chaos in our society and law is needed so the United States of America doesn't become dilapidated. We must restore our nation with a tutelary capacity so that we can be at our acme and have a plethora of jobs and maintain order of law so I present this ultimatum to the people of the United States of America which hopefully becomes a unanimity for all Americans.

What can you and I do to restore America to her former greatness as a united land of opportunity where each American can find a job and prosper? This book will exemplify the majority of problems and my book provides a solution. My knowledge and research is demonstrated here in the form of words so that the reader can take initiative to restore the United States of America to her proper state where everyone has an opportunity to prosper. You can actually participate in society by creating more jobs for United States citizens by reading this book and asking questions.

If you look at the vicissitudes in America, listen to your friends and fellow workers and if you are lucky enough to have a job and trust your feelings, you will believe in the truth of what this book provides.

Only when more people are willing to become involved like the concerned citizens who have helped with this book; will America once more become powerful.

Table of Contents

About the Author.................................

Introduction..

Chapter

. 1 American Workers in the United States.........

. 2 Your Vehicle.......................................

. 3 In My Home Area..............................

. 4 Gun Regulations and Society.....................

. 5 Creating Jobs in America.........................

. 6 Conserving Fuel and Time.......................

. 7 The American.....................................

. 8 Local, State, and Federal Government..........

. 9 Finding Work.....................................

. 10 Black-American Organizations..................

. 11 Schools and Students............................

. 12 Senior Citizens of America and Foreigners.....

ABOUT THE AUTHOR

I'm Derrick Frohne and was born April 16, 1985 in Saint Pete-Florida, USA. I am a great great grandson of Karl Elsener, the inventor of the Swiss Army Knife. I am also the son of Ralph Frohne and Judy Frohne. My siblings are Brandon Frohne, Holden Frohne, and Jesse Richardson. I grew up in Tennessee and moved back to Florida when I became 18. I worked in my family's Swiss-German-French restaurant for many years before I decided to study at University of South Florida. I became and author during my university studies and now I am the brand owner and manufacturer of the Gentle Bees brand. Gentle Bees is a brand naturak skin care products, beeswax aromatherapy wax melts, wood conditioner, and leather conditioner products I started in 2014. Gentle Bees brand has customers in USA, Canada, Mexico, United Kingdom, and Germany. This entire book and company started with a humble beginning.

INTRODUCTION

As I travel around in cyber space or in person asking others, I can see that America is a continuous vicissitude with so much unemployment and high interest rates where the average American family cannot buy a nice home or almost anything else. I see the many ways the large multi-national American companies are stealing from the American people and most of the American people not doing anything about this vicissitude. I have noticed how the American people have allowed many foreign countries to come to America and steal from the American people with all types of unfair practices, all for them and practically nothing for America simultaneously. The American people still are not doing anything about these practices either. Society will undergo a shift that will be uncanny unless we repair it soon. There will be so much criminal activity because of our own dilapidated thoughts. I ponder when America will awaken from her sleep, probably when it is too late.

Will all you allegiant Americans and United States future citizens reading the book I wrote stand up and let your opinion matter because you deserve it. As I have said many times before and as you and I both know, there is a very high degree of unemployment. Now, the United States of American is a beautiful, advanced country, industrialized country, and is an educated country. Now, could I ask you a simple question? How did this happen in this beautiful country? We are supposed to be the best in the world. I was indecisive however not sure so are we the best in the world? I believe the number one reason for all this unemployment is foreign imports. We Americans allow most other countries to bring their foreign products here to our beautiful country to sell them here in America, but those same foreign people pay very little or no import duty here in America. How did we allow this to happen? When we American manufacture products her in America and ship or fly them to those countries, we have to pay a very high import duty there? Is this a fair trade law? Some countries allowed to ship their products here absolutely free and at the same time we pay a high import duty for our products in their countries. Is that playing fair with us Americans? Quite the majority of the big American manufacturing companies have close factories or plants here in America an put Americans out in the streets with no jobs, put them on unemployment or welfare line and you and I have to support them. Then they turn right around and take those machines or build new ones in the foreign country. Then they sell their product with their name on it in the United States. Many are big manufacturing companies producing automobiles, steel, radio, televisions, toys, novelties, clothes, textiles, and especially shoes. We seldom make any shoes here in American anymore. They turn right around and ship that product right back here to American. Remember you are out there in the streets, unemployed and on welfare. You are laid off; they closed the factory or plant where you were working.

Now here is the benevolent part. As Americans you can go and buy that same product that you used to make a few months ago. The majority of the large department stores sell a large assortment of products shipped from other countries on ships and not on American ships with American flags. They make it there then ship it from there to America, and you as the American consumer unfortunately go to buy that foreign product. You don't take time to look at the label to see if it's made in the USA. That's the United States of America, the most beautiful country in the world. This is still America, so please think logically. I would not mind trade with those foreign people if it were on some kind of fair basis. They just set up some little old sweat shop over there some place, and they work the hell out of their people for practically nothing. They don't have an abundance of safety laws, they just build the product any way they can get it over to sell to you, and Americans buy the same foreign product that made a few months ago. Now you have put yourselves in the street. Now you are putting yourselves further in the streets on unemployment and welfare lines buy buying more of these foreign products. Very soon you will run out of unemployment or welfare.

Where will you go from there, on a soup line like in the depression? Now you may think this can't happen in the beautiful country. Well, let me set you straight. It is getting very close and all you have to do is listen to the news, read a newspaper, or listen to all of those Americans that have been laid off and are looking for a job, and then you will know. All you have left is to take that old gun you bought, probably foreign-made and rob your fellow American. Now don't be surprised to learn that he is also out there trying to rob you. He has been buying those foreign products also and he has probably been laid off also. Please let me repeat myself because Americans have bought so many of these products that it has become the main reason there is so much unemployment here in this beautiful country of the United States of America. They said they were doing you a favor.

You know that the government continuously lying in your face with TV and newspaper advertisements saying we don't want to raise the import duty on foreign products because it would cost you American too much here. Those foreign employees don't pay even one cent income tax here in America, not one cent social security tax here in America, not one cent employment insurance tax here in America, no state taxes, no gasoline or cigarette tax, and no other taxes here in America. Absolutely nothing here in America to help you and I so how can these great Americans buy foreign made products? How do those people figure that it is cheaper for you to buy those foreign products here? In The United States, you can't afford to accept that product for free. Remember, you are out in the street. You used to build it and now you are unemployed. The only way you can accept that foreign product is to accept it for free then destroy it. Tear it up and break it until it is completely destroyed. That is the only way that you as good Americans can accept a foreign product. Later when those same people come back to deal with Americans on a fair basis, one on one, they can charge eleven percent and we can charge eleven percent. That would be fair not like now where everything is for them and little for us.

At the moment, all you Americans go to buy a product here in USA, make sure it was made here in the United States of America. Every day and every night when you are awake, be American, buy American, and live American. Then eventually those foreign products will pile up on the docks or pile up in a warehouse and rot. It won't work if you aren't using it, so they will have to destroy it or take it back where they found it. Then those jobs will come back to USA because the market is still here in USA. It should not have reached this acme of unemployment, unstable interest rates, with all of our money going to these foreign countries and nothing staying here in the USA.

You bought their foreign products and now you have bought yourself out of a job here in America. Do you think those people will help you? No way will they help you, they are not stupid. They think if you are stupid to buy then you need no help. The crime rate will rise and you might need your guns just to protect yourself, but it might not happen if you just stop buying and investing in foreign products. Eventually those jobs will come back to the United States of America where they belong.

CHAPTER 1
AMERICAN WORKERS
IN THE UNITED STATES

This part of the book pertains to the American worker here in the United States of America. I think when a man works he has to work for a salary to pay his bills at home, such as a mortgage, car payments, food, and clothing for his family. When one is hired for a company, he must produce enough labor for that company to make profit over and beyond operating expense, plus his salary, so he must have great productivity or the corporation can't flourish. For example, if that company is only making, say $10 on labor and they have to pay you $20. That will make you go broke in quickly unless you pay $10 and they pay $20 then they can stay in business and can afford to pay you. Take into consideration that he has to pay much more than just your salary. He has to maintain an office force, buildings, transportation, and etc. When that company does make money off your labor and sweat, I believe that part of that money is rightfully yours, and it should come back to you: not going all one way, like if a company is making, say $50 and only giving you $2. That's not fair because you can't afford to buy the products that he manufactures. If he also is not making enough money, he can't buy anything. In the end, you have a lot of products with no takers, like it is beginning to be here in America, with all of those low salaried laborers in foreign countries making our products. In the very near future, there will not be a market here in America, or in those foreign countries, simply because no one is making a salary whereby they can afford those same products. I believe the American worker can produce just as good as any other worker in the world. We also have a good standard of living, because each worker here in the United States of America has to pay into a variety of benefits and all kinds of taxes such as income taxes, social security taxes, local, and state taxes to support your country here in America. If it was like it is in most of the foreign countries where you don't have to pay many taxes or none at all, they you could hire these same American at less than half of what you have to pay them now.

You wouldn't have an America anymore because who could support the government her in America? Are you stupid enough to believe those foreign people would support your government? No way, and when you become old and wanted to retire, then what? When you get laid off, who is going to pay your unemployment compensation? No tax from these foreign people, remember? Also, most Americans pay into some kind of health plan. If you or your family gets sick, who is going to pay for this if you are not working or paying taxes? Also, most Americans pay into some kind of pension plan. If no one is paying into these plans, how are you going to retire when you get old? Also, when you as American are not working, you are actually a drain on yourself and the government. At the time you are not working, you are not paying anything into the system, though you are taking out of the system. Some don't see how American workers can go out and buy all of those foreign products produced by foreign people. When they buy those products, they are simply buying themselves out of a job, and out of any benefits that they hope to get in the future. In most of the large chain department store, hardware stores, shoe stores, etc, you will see a large amount of products for sale that are made in some foreign country. I can't see how this can be. When they sell enough foreign products, that same store put Americans out of work. Actually they are only selling themselves out of the market her in America. I also believe that the average American working man evidently don't know what rights they have under the constitution of the United States of America.

We have freedom of speech but as these different factories and plants close down here in the United States, I don't see many people saying much about it. Also we have the right to assembly. I don't see anybody putting up protest lines around those same plants and factories. We have also freedom of the press. I don't see too much print about this practice or how to go about curing this problem. They keep on closing down factories and plants here in America, simply because the American people just keep buying foreign products that Americans used to make a short time ago. Maybe you think when you buy a product that you don't make that particular product, but when you buy that foreign product, you are putting some other American out of a job.

Eventually he can't buy the product that you make or sell, so when you buy that foreign product, you are actually putting you own self out of a job. For example, you make or sell refrigerators, and you are driving a foreign car or pickup to go back and forth to work or to deliver that same refrigerator. That same foreign car put one American family out of work for about one year. When enough people here in America buy enough of those foreign machines, and then they will not be employed so they can't buy that refrigerator you sell. You will be out of a job simply because you bought that foreign machine in the first place. The American people are going to have to start to understand what is really happening here in America because if they don't, the situation is going to get worse. It is not going to get any better. The American people must stand up for their rights and be counted. Let's stop closing all of the plants and factories here in America and let America know that we as Americans will not tolerate this practice any longer. A lot of people think it is the government's fault

Don't you know that you are the government? It is not the government's fault.

No one twisted your arm and made you buy those foreign products. You did it on your own, so don't go complain to the government. They can't help you, when you don't help yourselves. I know they have a very small import duty on those foreign products, but I don't see any protest lines around the docks where they bring them into the United States of America. I also don't see any American protest lines around foreign embassies in foreign countries. Also, in our capital in Washington D. C, these same countries have many people in high places, making extremely high salaries, to work for the foreign countries promoting foreign products. A majority of these people who are working for foreign countries used to work for our interests in our capital. Now they are selling out to the highest bidder.

These types of people should be arrested if that's possible, because they are actually selling the Americanworker down the river to foreign powers. Actually Americans should try to get to our representatives in Washington, and try to get to our representatives in Washington, and try to get some kind of quotas on foreign products. I really don't know if that will do any good, as it has been tried before and it didn't work. You really don't know how will sell you out to the highest bidder. Maybe we Americans have only one way to go, and that is to take the matter our own hands and handle the problems ourselves before it gets so bad we won't' have anything to protect. In the near future, there won't be too much industry here in America at all because at the present time they are closing plant, factories, banks, and businesses at an alarming rate. This can't continue without grave results to Americans. All anyone has to do is just listen to the news or read any paper, and they will know what is happening here in America. The unemployment rate is so high it can't be allowed to go any higher without a complete collapse of the American system then what will happen? A complete depression will happen so please understand this.

When the unemployed get ahead of the employed, the foreign products get ahead of American products, like it is today in America, there is only one way to go and that is out. When you are unemployed and still buying foreign products, naturally there is nothing going into the system so it has to collapse. As any industry closes down, it also takes many more industries down with it, such as supply houses office equipment machinery, restaurant services, etc. It can wipe out a whole city at once. All of the feeder industries such as plastics, rubber, glass, paint sheet metal, steel, etc go out also. The local government relies on the workers to support the schools, police departments, hospitals, parks, and libraries. Naturally, when no funds are coming into these departments, they have to cut back funding or close the department. Then what? It is really hard to find anything made in America anymore. They probably figure we Americans are so dumb that they can sell us anything. Little do those companies know that they are really destroying the best market in the world? When there are so many Americans out of work, they won't be able to sell American or foreign products here in the United States of American anymore. These American companies try just about every trick in the trade. They get a box with Made in USA on it then they put a foreign product in it. The box costs 15 cents but the foreign product could cost hundreds or even thousands of dollars but Americans buy it and do not look at it closely.

Also, some of the large chain stores have a habit of putting a sign on their merchandise stating that the merchandise is sold by that particular company, but they don't say where it was made. We have definitely got to get laws on the books to make those people put on their merchandise where it was actually made. Then we will know whether to buy it or leave it alone. Please Americans, be good Americans. But totally American, ship American fly American, live American, and bank American. If this is done, the problems we have in the United States will go away with the recession and we can restore our country again.

CHAPTER 2 YOUR VEHICLE

Every time you see a foreign car on the streets or highways of this country or in your neighbor's garage or maybe even in your own garage, that car represents one average American family out of work for a year. After buying that car and paying interest on a loan for the car, the total cost will come to an average of $10,000. That's the equivalent of about $400 a week in take home pay. That's money that doesn't stay here but goes overseas to the foreign car manufacturer. This money that leaves our economy and the money that could have kept an American employed for one year, so that American and his or her family could live and pay their bills for one year.

Instead that money has gone to a foreign company with foreign employees who pay no taxes here in this country. They add no funds to our unemployment insurance plans or our social security system. Maybe that car was a little cheaper than an equivalent American automobile. However, buying that foreign car has put Americans out of work or maybe even himself. He has decreased his chances of getting benefits from his government now or in the future.

Americans have bought so many foreign products over the years that thousands of American factories and companies have closed.

Entire industries are threatened or have almost disappeared. Unemployment is the highest it has been since the great depression. We must do something to avoid another depression in this country, or we will experience an economic collapse even greater than that of the 1930s. Americans must stop buying foreign products, particularly foreign cars, if our economy is to survive.

The taxes the Americans are not paying are nothing to what the foreign car companies and other manufacturers are not paying. They make goods over there, sell them here, and then take back all the money to their own country. That's billions of billions of dollars. The way they drain our economy make the money Americans don't report look like petty cash. Nobody from the government wants to admit the real truth about why our economy is abating but I have. At least the money American make through outside incomes stay in the United States whether or not they pay taxes on it unless they buy foreign cars with it.

Just within the last few years, we had to bail out GM Corporation from a hole they largely made. Now they are probably taking the tax dollars we gave them to Japan where they are building many of the so called American cars to reduce the cost for the company. The results are even more American auto workers will be out of jobs. All the big car manufacturers make cars outside the country. Ford motor company has their most advanced assembly plant not in the United States but in Brazil. Ford also is investing over 449 million in Thailand for a plant to be built and Ford will give around 2,100 jobs to foreign people. This plant will take away 2,100 jobs for American workers since the company is overseas. We need more plants from Ford like the one in Chicago where it has remained in business since 1929. The money the carmaker earns from sales can stay in the United States of America and can promote job stability to local residents by giving them consistent work. Fortunately Ford didn't accept any government bailout money so they could take this money and go overseas with it and make more plants to take away jobs for Americans.

GM has received more than 49 billion dollars in bailout money taken from the taxpayers although the company slashed thousands of jobs in America. How can they do that to the Americans who bailed them out? This is uncanny to think that the GM Company would do such a thing. It's like sticking a knife into your mother's back after she fed you and gave you a house to live in. GM also has considered sending billions of dollars overseas so they can make plants there. It's very interesting to see how quick they become traitors to the American taxpayers who worked for them. First, they take the taxpayers' money who worked for them in the United States then they lay them off without work then have meetings about where they want to make plants in foreign countries. This money was to protect Americans and their economy. This shows that the government bailout has done nothing to stabilize the economy in the United States. GM made an announcement in 2009 saying that they were laying off more than 3,398 workers on salary in the United States. They have more than 24,899 salary workers at the moment. Chrysler also made a statement that they have cut about 24.9 percent or 5,000 white collar workers.

They also announced more than 788 dealerships which will be closed in the United States and this means more Americans are without work because of their bankruptcy in 2009. That is more than 24 percent of their plants which are inside the United States of America. The dealers which will be closed represent more approximately 13.9 percent of their sales. The United States Treasury Department lost a lot of money in the bailout of Chrysler. They lost more than 1.5 billion from the 4 billion they were given in the bailout. Chrysler has repaid their 1.9 billion dollars so far. After the government gets 500 million which is promised, Chrysler will only be in deficit 1.6 billion dollars. To make our economy even worse, Chrysler had 85 million dollars in legal fees for their bankruptcy case and guess who pays these fees? The American taxpayer pays the fees. The total debt will depend after the United States government sells their share from the Chrysler.

We should never alter the free market or give anymore bailouts. People are impetuous because they want to see results quick but it is not worth to see anymore bankruptcy cases from automakers. We need tax breaks for American workers to bring these jobs back to America so Americans can have stability once again.

The big problem is not foreigners or the government. The real problem is you and I. We deserve what we have done for buying these foreign cars, a lot of Chevy plants have been closed by the Japanese, German, and Korean carmakers. Tennessee has enticed Volkswagen to construct a manufacturing plant in Chattanooga for tax breaks which costs around 576 million dollars. In 2005, the state lured Nissan to relocate their headquarters from California by giving over 197 million dollars in incentive including more than 19 million dollars in savings for utility bills. In 1992, South Carolina has taken a BMW plant for 150 million USD in giveaways. You probably think that Japanese cars sell better her just because they are cheaper and that's because we are suckers. Our government has been outmaneuvered and doesn't do a thing about it. If Japanese cars entering this country were subjected to the same restrictions the Japanese place on our cars going into their country, your Honda or Toyota would cost twice as much. There wouldn't be many available either at any price because the Japanese have import quotas on American cars. So the Japanese keep our cars out by a lot of restrictive laws. By the time they slap on import duty, excise taxes, and a variety of other costly taxes, permits, and procedures, our cars will be another 100 percent to sell. On the other hand, we charge the Japanese only 2-3 percent on taxes to bring the cars into our country. So our government, with the cooperation of us, the people hits our auto industry and economy with a one-two punch. We let the Japanese get away with their outrageous import charges so that our automobile companies are able to sell only a very few cars in Japan. We allow them to come into our country at almost no extra charge. The result is hundreds and thousands of U.S auto workers out of jobs, four times as many more people in related jobs out of work, and a trade deficit of more than 44.6 million dollars in 2009 with Japan. This means that America spent more 44.6 million dollars more for Japanese products than they did for our.

So that's 44.6 million dollars going away from our economy and this strengthens the Japanese economy. The stronger they are, the better they'll be about to drain us financially. We are directly responsible for the unemployment and financial problem of this country. Look around the street and parking lots in this country and you will see that approximately 60 percent of the cars are foreign make. We sold out a long time ago and now it's creating many problems now as the Americans are observing the problems now. Not only have we sold our soul for foreign good, but we even use foreign ships to bring them here so we have managed to sweep out our maritime industry. You will never see a foreign car arrive here on a ship flying a United States flag. Our government could require goods come here on U.S ships so that we would at least get a little money out of the deal. Our maritime industry, an instant Navy in time of war, is now almost nonexistent. We would end up losing in a hundred different ways. What can we do about it? We can place an embargo on Korean, German, Italian, and Japanese cars. There are various things that can be done. I suggest we Americans stop buying foreign cars right now. Let's start protecting our economy and assisting ourselves and our American citizens so they can get their jobs back. Let's get America back on the track again and help it be the strong independent country it once was. It all starts with you and your willingness to say no more foreign products. Look at your television, which is probably made in Japan or China. I should plan to set up a foundation in the future called, The American Research to Cure the Foreign Plague. Trash receptacles can be situated all over America where Americans can junk foreign made products that are ruining our economy and putting our workers in unemployment lines.

Automobiles imported from Japan are the worse threat to our economy and American employment because there are so many of them and they drain million of dollars from our economy which could create jobs for American citizens. Each time you see a Nissan or Toyota on our streets, you see an entire American family out of a job for a year. I say an entire family because that car will cost about 22 thousand dollars. Many American workers with families to support barely make that in a year. What can we do about this problem? Let's start with the Nissan Company. They had a slogan that says they are driven. Well, it's a great slogan; however, let's utilize that same slogan to destroy them in the United States. Let's say you have bought a Nissan but are out of work and can't make payments. Simply drain the oil from the engine and replace the drain plug. Watch the commercials advertising Japanese or Chinese products. It should make you mad enough to throw away that TV and every other foreign made product you own. We can't blame Japan, China, or other foreign nations, or our government because we are the government. We can be number one in the television industry and the auto industry again. Tell yourself that you are buying American made products from now on and stop buying the foreign made products

CHAPTER 3
IN MY HOME AREA

A t the moment in 2010, I live in Saint Pete-Florida and there are thousands of foreign cars remaining stationary in the lots. Foreign car corporations are sending these cars here at very fast because they are probably afraid that our government will start raising the import duty. We should write the State of Florida many letters and protest against foreign products. What would be funny is if someone drove a Toyota or Nissan to do these protests that prohibit the cars from entering our ports. Now, I want to talk about foreigners who come to Tampa Bay area for jobs and schools. These foreigners come into our nations and take jobs away from the American Citizens.

I have experienced this for myself when I have been inside the University of South Florida on both campuses in Saint Pete and Tampa, I have seen majority of foreign workers. I don't understand how our government officials or school officials can give more jobs to people who don't have the same rights as we Americans have. Americans must be first here in the United States of America. We should be entitled to have jobs before foreigners. I have spoken with a student who said that most foreigners he knows just come here to study and work. He also mentioned that the United States government issues credit cards to them and they can just buy what they want and go back home to foreign soil without paying for their debt while being in the United States. This annoys me a lot because imagine how many could be doing this to our beautiful nation which we Americans live for and die for. These foreigners should pay for their debt overseas with interest if they want to go back home. There must be a new law that says their debt follows them no matter where they go after departing the United States.

Next, Saint Petersburg College has some qualities that are not appealing to the American economy and way of life. The President of Saint Petersburg College has helped bring foreign students here to work in place of American students. I met a lot of the Russian international students and they visited with the President of the College. They said he is a very nice man. Yes, I am sure he is a nice man, however, in my opinion not to the American students. He gives them priority over Americans which is a bad economical policy. I understand he wants to bring more international students here and that's fine but to give them jobs before American students is preposterous. That's like saying, I will help you American students with education but you can forget having a job here. A rising number of those foreigners are buying homes now at low costs and little to no restrictions to them. They know that our economy is abating and they can make more money on buying properties rather than buying some type of stock. They can rent these properties and make a great profit so they can continue to buy more properties. Recently, luxurious condos in downtown Miami had announced they already sold over 261 units out of the 372 units within the complex and almost 89 percent of the units were bought by foreigners who paid cash. They made that money from you and me because we are buying foreign products. Also, Miami has more people who speak Spanish than English. On my recent vacation to Miami to visit my friend Joel Diaz, I noticed that every store I enter has people who speak Spanish and not English. I felt like a foreigner in the United States. I tried to ask some people at a convenient store for help at finding vitamins and they didn't understand me but fortunately my friend was there to translate.

Orlando has been an appealing place for foreigner to come over and buy homes, especially people from the United Kingdom. The average home dropped to around 100,000 USD or approximately 64,000 British Pounds. The British foreigners are buying not older homes but newer homes because the prices are so affordable. Three additional states are luring foreigners to buy here in the United States. Texas, California, and Arizona along with Florida accounted for 53 percent of the sales of homes to foreign buyers with 15 percent of buyers buying homes over 500,000 USD and more than 54 percent are paying with cash. Now we should continue to sell these homes to them in hope that they buy a business here or create a business for Americans since they now live here. This could help stimulate the economy.

There are so many opportunities for America that we can do. Go after Avis and Hertz and Avis car rentals and make them buy only American Cars by passing legislation in Congress by lobbyists and other political nationalists of the United States of America. Help me force legislation that says that they must refuse loans for foreign cars. You must explain to Bank of America that it is in their best interest to help create job for America. Let them know that you when people ask who you bank with, they say, I bank America.

Bring your Nissan, Toyota, or other Chinese products and destroy them in a public demonstration however, you might need to get a special permit for it. In fact do it in the front of the Japanese or Chinese consulate or nearest trade office. We are losing our robust economy all because of you and I. We must restore our power; we must restore our great nation. We have struggled a lot; however, we can make our homeland robust again with your help. We are the one, so let's go to work.

CHAPTER 4
GUN REGULATIONS
AND SOCIETY

I have written this letter in the form of a chapter to speak the thoughts of many Americans who don't want to challenge authority; however, I will challenge authority to the end for the people of the United States of America. I serve my nation well by writing this letter addressing my concerns. The first concern of the people of the United States is gun control. It is not in our nation's best interest to be disarmed. We the people exercise our rights for protection provided in the United States Constitution. These are the same laws that protect us and give us the right to have weapons. Some people disagree with the constitution and they think we shouldn't have the right to own guns. They are the same people who tried to stop the country from drinking during Prohibition. At that time, there were more people drinking during the prohibition than before the prohibition laws were enforced.

When gun are outlawed, only people who are outlaws will have guns. If you remove the guns from law- abiding citizens, the people who will have guns are the many who will not think twice to shoot you. Americans will protest even if the government attempts to remove our right to own guns. Next, the people who support gun control say that if the laws are passed then everyone will have to give their guns to the government. If Congress passes a law that Americans couldn't buy guns anymore that sure would not stop the foreigners from making them. They are already equipped to make them and they will not close their shops because of the new law or laws in our society. The foreigners are not naïve and they know how to market their guns to any nation that wants to buy them.

Those people all over the world who buy them will know that Americans can't own guns anymore. After the find out that we are weak and unarmed, they will bring their guns over here and use them on us. We won't have any way to defend ourselves. What will we do then? Throw sand in their face or throw a smile to them. Also, National Rifle Association, you work together with the Veterans of foreign wars. Those members of the VFW are veterans because they fought some of the foreigners who manufacture the guns we buy today. We should educate our children with guns and inform them about our rights to own guns and why owning a gun is so valuable. We must remain neutral and detached so they know all about gun history.

I want to see my children and grand-children in the future protected and the only way we can do it is to continue to own guns and our gun industry also. We must stop buying foreign guns and start restoring our own industry for American citizens.

These people who want to outlaw guns recognize that the American economy is abating and will soon become a depression. There are millions of people out on the street who are unemployed and they know the reasons so many people are committing crime with guns are that they are trying to obtain money to support their family. They are desperate so they utilize a gun as a last option because they do not visualize another way out. Law-abiding United States citizens think that if guns are outlawed there are no more problems, albeit people need to still support their family.

We the people still need to find jobs for ourselves again with good pay and benefits. There are not many jobs left and American companies have closed because we all buy foreign products which include; cars, guns, clothes, televisions, and etc.

If the National Rifle Association wants to accumulate more money to lobby with and make sure gun control always are not passed, you must tell your friends, family, co-workers, and other acquaintances of my book and tell them to read it so it will alleviate their stress and help you significantly. You can take this book and lobby with it in Congress because our laws need to remain the same way. Another plan I have in mind is The American Research to Cure the Foreign Plague. We have a very bad case of the foreign plague her in the United States of America. Probably half of your organization is driving around in Toyota, Subaru, BMW, or Nissan cars and shooting foreign guns.

There should be some type of rebate plan for giving them away and then they should be replaced. The foreign guns should be replaced with American guns, made from the steel of the old foreign guns. If everybody who owns a foreign gun has done this, then we could start making a lot more American guns and create more jobs for America and her children. If you have members who are gun dealers with shops in foreign lands, please tell them to come back home to the United States of America to create more jobs and they can use this money to buy the products they make and can support their family with the money they earn from your gun members. These American dealers who are making factories in other countries are traitors of their own nation, the United States of America. They will not be forced to rob you because they need money to support their family. They will have jobs again after some of your gun members come back home and we would not need gun control laws when this becomes a reality.

There is another topic that I want to explain. There are guns which police departments use and I have seen police motorcycles not made in the United States of America. Police officers also have weapons that are made in a foreign land. These police officers spend half their time making our neighborhoods safe by using their guns on people who had to result to criminal act in order to survive and to provide food for his or her family. They don't have jobs because they have bought foreign products and that is why these law-abiding citizens have killed to assure their survival.

The Police who go after these people are using foreign guns, tasers, handcuffs, and even motorcycles. Some of these people who are committing crimes are teenagers and they don't appreciate the consequences of their actions. In society today, the police are utilizing soft and hard technologies to effectively deal with juveniles in society today while jobs are being lost and society is slowly becoming worse. The soft technology includes information technology systems to ameliorate police administrative and operational decision making such as: deployment of resources to crime havens and analysis of crime patterns. Some of the tantalizing hard technologies of today include the following: stun guns, tasers, and mace.

The police forces are also utilizing surveillance systems for deterrence against juvenile delinquents in society. Community policing is another great method because the police officers become familiar with the people and neighborhoods therefore, their policing becomes more effective. Another method of effective policing for juveniles is the presence of police officers in grade schools. Police can become familiar with the students so they can build trust in each other. The officer in grade schools usually acts as a social service model which would represent the best interest of the juvenile offender. Having discretion toward juveniles should be taken into consideration because we were all young and at the young tender age, the mind is not developed entirely and these juveniles make mistakes because they are either inebriated or just don't understand the consequences of their actions.

There are many qualities that people can posses that will handle juvenile cases more fairly and faster. Because of the current situation with everyone losing jobs, I think that community policing is a great quality to possess as a police department entity. Community policing helps in many ways because the main police role will be to increase feelings of community safety and make it where the local residents are working together with the police officer or officers. This is also good because the police officers can trust these juveniles more and in return they do not feel they need to arrest the same juvenile for committing a crime.

These crimes that juveniles make could be the result of physical, emotional, or mental violence and if the police know that, they can try to provide a rehabilitation model for the juveniles. Everyone just wants to be loved and have attention so if the police can offer some type of assistance by being involved then this would help significantly. Juvenile officers work either as specialists in a police department or in a juvenile unit of a police department. They must possess a huge quantity of the law, especially the protections made by the constitution available to juveniles. The people who will work with juveniles must go through extensive training with dealing with aggressive juveniles. Handling these juvenile offenders can produce major role conflicts for police. They will experience a tension between their zeal to make what they think is the primary job duty, law enforcement, and the zeal to help rehabilitate the juvenile offenders.

Judges will use discretion when sentencing females for murder during these detrimental times and the popular method of discretion is the chivalry theory. The chivalry theory says that women are not executed as much because we the men are supposed to protect them and that's why they are not sentenced to death as much as males. The percentage of death row inmates who are females are less than three percent. Women commit felony homicides as much as men, albeit they are not executed as much for the crime.

I know the police probably don't make the decision where their weapons and motorcycles are made and who they are bought from. That is for the City and State Government to do. It is time that everyone sees that we can't buy guns made overseas anymore and when we start refusing to buy those guns and buy only American made guns, we will create more jobs and have more Americans working again and the American police will not need to use their guns as much.

CHAPTER 5 CREATING JOBS IN AMERICA

I know many ways to create jobs here in the United States of America and you can assist too. You can start by finding someone who needs the assistance. You might know somebody who does not have work. If not, just call the unemployment or welfare offices or go in person to the office. There will be many people out of work there. You have a responsibility to help your neighbors, allies, and friends. When your brother is down, you must give a helping hand to help him. I will bet you have some things around your home that you need help with whether it is painting, tile, carpentry, roofing, landscaping, or painting. Go buy the items needed for the job, however, make sure that they are made in the United States of America. This book is made for the sole purpose of creating jobs for American citizens in America and not foreigners. American consumers who buy foreign products have made this trouble for our nation. The next step is to find one or two unemployed Americans who could be your neighbors or family. Tell the person that you want to hire him or her for a project. Tell this person just one more thing. Say that he or she must give you something made in a foreign land

that you own. After the foreign product is brought to you, then destroy it. You must say that you are hiring him or her because he or she is American and that all Americans must stay together and help each other and make sure that we buy only American products. I went into Lowes and also Home Depot to find American wire cutters. I finally found some wire cutters made in USA.

You give him or her job until the project is done and make sure that you say that you are not mad at him or her for buying items made on foreign land. Oh by the way, I have some of them myself. We as Americans don't have to be ignorant anymore because we know how much buying foreign products effect us in the United States the only way to bring the United States to her back to a robust nation is to buy only American products made by American citizens. If you really want to help your neighbor, destroy your foreign car and your foreign TV. If one comes to your house to work for you, make sure they have tools made in the United States of America.

Finding American products are difficult. If they don't have tools made in the United States of America, ask him or her to leave the property until they have tools made in the United States of America. Also inform them that their clothes and shoes must be made in the United States of America. We need to remove the foreign plague which is destroying our way of life. I just want to see everyone with a job again. If every American in the United States would hire one more American to do some work, we could assist Americans even if it is only a few days. This work can buy a lot of groceries so to feed their family.

No man is a tropical island and we can't do this by ourselves. If we amalgamate our ideas, we can make a better future but when we don't then our economy will continue to abate then our US government might fly a different flag because of a foreign invasion. Now you are thinking what to do with all the foreign items you throw away. You can just destroy them and put them in trash cans and maybe in the future, our government will use the money from foreign import taxes to set-up the program so that all foreign products are recycled and then the products can be made in the USA with that logo. I understand we all make mistakes and we can fix this mistake. After reading this book, you will be educated enough to know why I have written this short novel and how it will become your savior to a better life.

CHAPTER 6
CONSERVING FUEL
AND TIME

There are different ways to save millions of gallons of fuel here in the United States of America. One does not need to rely on the Middle Eastern nations and members of OPEC. There are ways which we can secure our money here in our beautiful nation, the United States of America and not need to send our money to foreigners so they can come back here and buy up our land. Most states within New America have tolls where one stops immediately from 45 MPH to 0 MPH in the matter of seconds to wait in line burning gasoline and wait a minute or sometimes longer just to throw a couple coin in the box or to give money to the cashier. After the toll is paid, one must accelerate quickly to the set speed of 45 MPH or even fast depending on the road or highway. This uses a lot of gasoline to accelerate quickly to your average speed on the highway or road. It costs quite a lot for everyone to slow down at the tolls then to quickly accelerate again. It might be 2 ounces depending on what type of vehicle you are driving. This problem is worse for Trucks because they are hauling heavy loads for companies. These truckers have to stop which causes pain on the brakes because there is so much pressure. Also because these trucks have heavy weight the cost for fuel is much more when they need to accelerate quickly so you don't make a traffic jam.

I understand that the states rely on revenue for their infrastructure such as roads and bridges but a toll tax is not the best way to do make money for the states and it's not good for the air. There is so much pollution by all of these vehicles because they must accelerate quickly after paying the toll. I have already proposed to a state politician in Florida via email about just charging more in vehicle registration so that we can remove all toll gates. I think the majority of people would gladly pay an extra two dollars per year versus stopping at these tolls paying money and this costs Americans more money. We must be fiscal responsible because if not, we will destroy our economy much worse than it is today. We all have driven early in the morning and stop at the toll booth when the cashier was half awake and he didn't want to be there. I wrote Senator Bill Nelson and other congress member about my concerns with this issue and other issues and they responded with letters of interest.

The only way to have a job for everyone is to keep money in the United States of America. Also don't anything foreign and this will help create jobs for Americans. This is not a dream, it's reality and a vision that will come true and it is just a matter of time before the people understand that they must do a lot to stop buying foreign products and to reinstate the American jobs by bringing companies back to the United States of America.

I just want my book read and seen nationwide by American citizens so that people know to create jobs and where to find a job. I am for America and only America. I want only the best for my fellow Americans. After we close the tolls in the United States, we can save billions of gallons of fuel and we can slowly stop being dependent on foreign oil. The price will slowly decrease since the demand will be less. Let's stop using too much fuel by eliminating tolls. It is definitely not fair to close tolls in one state but not another. It must be done all together at a Federal level. We might need to start at a state level so that it provides an example of how much money and time will be saved. I say that we must flood you state and federal representatives' office with emails and letters until they realize this will benefit all Americans. Tell them that you want to pay the extra two dollars on your car registration rather than to stop and pay tolls. The quicker you write your representatives, the quicker we can become independent as a nation again. Most toll plazas are expensive to build and the taxpayer is the one paying for the expenses.

There are other ways to save on fuel. We can still save money on gasoline be just keeping a proper amount of air in your tires. Under-inflated tires are one the basic ignored causes bad fuel efficiency. Consider that most cars lose approximately 1 psi each month. Tires that are not properly inflated create roll resistance which means that the car needs more gas to make the car continue to run. Look at your tires one time monthly and when the temperature is at the lowest point of the day since operating the vehicle heats the tires and the air inside them. Another way to save fuel is to replace your air filter when dirty. Dirty air filters restrict the amount of air flow in the engine, which damages the fuel economy and performance. The air filters are actually easy to check and replace. Locate your user manual and see if there is a clogged filter. Usually people changed their air filter every 14,000 miles since it is a paper air filter. I would like to exemplify how you can save more money and time by replacing your air filter. Once it is time to replace your air filter, go buy a K&N air filter. This filter is a 1,000,000 mile air filter. Most engines function for 150,000 miles if properly maintained. People change their air filter 10 times on average during the ownership of that car this is a permanent air filter that never needs to be changed, however, only cleaned. This air filter must be cleaned every 60,000 miles so that saves you money and time. Next, eliminate using the air conditioner in your car. You can save up to ten percent on your vehicle fuel costs by not using your air conditioner. Make sure that you wash and clean your car because extra weight will decrease the fuel economy. Make sure that you don't accelerate fast because this costs more for fuel. Also make sure to tighten your gas cap because gasoline evaporates. Try to drive only in the cooler temperature because gasoline evaporates quicker in the hot temperature. Check and change your spark plugs if needed. A misfired spark plug can reduce the efficiency of the vehicle by 30 percent. One can use the correct type of oil recommended by the manufacturer to save between 1 and 2 percent on fuel.

CHAPTER 7 THE AMERICAN

When American parents give life to a kid in the United States of America, it is a moral obligation to protect and love the child, to make sure it has dental and medical assistance, and their main obligation is to teach that child at different stages of his or her life as a toddler, in Kindergarten, elementary school, middle school, high school, and during college how to be a great American here in the United States of America. They must be taught this so this will insure they will have happiness and a prosperous life. As parents, you all brought the child into existence and the child is your responsibility to care for until he or she reaches a specific age and can defend and make his or her path in life. When a child is born he or she is born ignorant unfortunately because the mind has not developed to its acme so the baby knows not what is right or wrong and doesn't know what to do. Your kids are all yours and you must teach them. Toddlers, children, and adults play with toys or electronics. Most of these toys are made in foreign lands such as China or Japan. Some of these corporations that make these toys or electronics are American corporations but they use foreign products and labor therefore marring the economy. For example, the Apple iPhone is assembled in China. The same parents here in the United States of America are out of work because they have bought so many foreign products which results in the closing of plants and factories here in the United States of America. A laconic sentence that people should remember is, just think America. If you search for American toys long enough, you will find them made in the United States of America. I have observed Americans don't care where the products are made. They want the product just because of an impulsive feeling or they want to compete against another so they can look important. The United States of America will not fix the problem until the last moment just like in most problems.

The people who suffer the most are the same children that should be taught when their mother and father are not working because they have bought an abundance of foreign products. The parents can't buy anything for their family anymore because they don't have a consistent source of income. They will be fortunate to pay a mortgage and put groceries in their home for a limited time. During the family's nadir they can think about how those foreign items marred their lives. If some of you obstinate Americans have taken the time to understand what it means by buying these foreign made items, you would still be employed here in the United States of America and you would be able to afford the great American dream and put money into the system for future benefits. During through your child or children's life they will need clothing so when you go to a clothing store you see many clothes are made in foreign lands and you should not buy them. There are still clothes made in the USA but you must search for them. They will cost more money than the Chinese products however to buy them will not put you, your family, or fellow Americans out of work. Those foreigners do nothing to help your family so why buy from them. Foreign fabrics are crafted into shirts, pants, socks, caps, sweaters, and jackets. They have also conquered American stores. If you don't believe me, go walk in many clothing stores and look at the products to see where they are made. There are a few clothing items still made in USA however you must search for them. If Americans buy their clothes made in

USA, then the economy can be rejuvenated. It is very simple, just buy American made products and bring companies back to the United States of America. There would be more jobs in the United States and you and your family can enjoy the great life. If you buy these foreign products, this teaches your children that it is a good idea to buy foreign products.

When they buy foreign products, American jobs are lost because of it. Go ahead, look at all your electronics, clothes, appliances, and your car. I can confidently make the statement and say that the majority of the items are made in foreign lands. I have proven my point again and I need to help you fix the problem. As you read my book, you can see how nettled I am with our economy and our buying habits. I understand Americans are inured to buying foreign products but we can't do that anymore. We need intrepid people to stand up and make this country robust again. My jingoism is why I am writing this book. I love the United States and I am proud to be an American and with this eloquent message you and I will rejuvenate this beautiful nation. I hope these words eloquent enough so you help me restore our nation. Attention, we are the people and we are the government, so let's reduce the amount of foreign products we buy. This can be done with the help of just one person. One person can mollify the people by sending a message to foreign companies. We will enervate their profits and build ours by being American.

Next, they will want to learn foreign languages not because their family speaks foreign languages but because they can get a job in a foreign country. If you continue to buy all these foreign products in the United States of America, eventually there will only a couple jobs left in our beautiful nation of USA. People will have a difficulty when deciding which language to learn because we have an abundance of items from different foreign nations. I think that parents have not been taught by their parents and that's why we can't allow this to happen to their children. We must teach them.

After the kids are grown up and search for a job and discover there are no jobs here, they will question what happened to America. They will find out the industry is in other foreign lands and not in the United States of America. The American children deserve more than this. After graduating from high school or the university, some can't find a job. You can't blame them for being lethargic when there are no jobs because you are the one who bought all those foreign products putting your children out of jobs at this moment and in the future. When they see six or seven people experience waiting in line for a job, they will ask what has happened. I can see that America is going to have a young revolution to handle very soon and these children no matter what age will need answers and if they don't receive answers, they will come looking for you and I. They cannot be blamed since we never taught them and never gave them guidance.

All children require some type of guidance from their parents but unfortunately you have not given them guidance. I believe the children will need to teach their parents because something must be done soon. Things are not becoming better, they are becoming worse. We need to help bring jobs back to America, so one can live the American way. We need to create factories and plants here in the United States of America and bring back factories to the USA so all Americans have the chance to have a good stable job and support themselves and families.

It seems that most Americans were not taught by their family what America represents because the America is not doing well with high rising unemployment rates and high oil prices, gas prices, car insurance prices, health insurance prices, and property taxes. First I want to speak about unemployment rates. Unemployment rates in Florida are absurd. In the month of December, the unemployment rate was 11.8 percent which was super close to breaking the all time record set approximately 35 years ago. At a national level, labor participation abated to a 24 year low in the month of December of 2009. Approximately 1.7 million American citizens went away from the work force between the months of July and December and was the most detrimental six month decrease since the year 1961.

Oil prices have remained stationary for the past year between 70-85 dollars each barrel. The oil economy has stabilized and came back to a more normal shape after many years of abnormal prices and crazy conditions. The oil market today has surplus capacity in all parts of the business, abating for the potential of prices spikes. There has been a slight fluctuation in oil prices however we don't need to continue with foreign oil. We don't want to set a bad example for our children. For those people who are already parents, you understand my concerns and frustrations with oil. It cause problems with the ozone layer and also makes problems for everyone. Coal and oil consist of carbon and hydrogen and destroy our atmosphere. The carbon dioxide that coal produces causes the greenhouse effect. I hope this informs you and will help you think about these greenhouse gases because your children and their children will be alive even if you are not and they must breathe this air. Do you want your children, grand children, great grand children, and great great grand children to live in times where acid rain kills anything it contacts or the air is so bad; the people need respirators to breathe? This can happen to your children in the future so let us do something about it now. I have already started by working with Cadmium Telluride solar cells. Solar energy is a great source of energy because the sun produces clean energy needed for us and our children.

I have been working with Cadmium Telluride solar cells since year 2009 and my team and I are trying to make the solar cells more efficient and more affordable so everyone can enjoy clean and affordable energy directly from their house without contacting the power company for assistance. We still have a long way to go before solar panels can produce all the energy we need, but I see the future in my mind and it is clear that we will have clean, efficient, and affordable energy in the future. We have no other options. I know that I want to build a house here in Florida eventually after I am finished with my studies where I can have solar panels on my house to produce all the energy needed for my electric. I also want to build a solar hot water heater since this is the way to go. The technology is almost there and now just need to wait for the prices to decline.

I live in the United States of America and see a future for the people. The future consists of people buying or building houses with solar panels on their roof. The price for this can be adjusted within the mortgage so one can have clean and efficient energy. There should actually be a law that mandates all new houses must come with small non-grid solar systems so that we can reduce our dependence on foreign oil, natural gas, or coal. With the new non-grid solar systems, we can live much better without the worry of our electric company making a profit from us. The United States Government must stop giving oil companies so many leniencies so they can charge the average American a lot of money for their services. We can start doing this now. Write your legislator explaining why Solar and Wind energy are so important. Once their offices are flooded with these letters, they will address the concerns but we must not stop there. We must go through the media in newspapers and TV with our hope for the future. Our children will live in this world and when they do, I want them to be safe and to live a prosperous life.

Next, car insurance rates are continuing to rise as our children are growing older. Some people have experience rising rates without filing a claim. Most of the insurance premiums are passed on to our new drivers who are our children and we get stuck paying the bill unless they have a job. I want to see that our children know how to work and value their money so they can take be responsible to handle their own car insurance.

Remember to eschew all foreign products so you and your family can live the American dream.

CHAPTER 8
LOCAL, STATE, AND FEDERAL GOVERNMENT

There are a lot of problems that happened in different levels of the government. You can relate because there are problems that your city government, your state, and your federal government are experiencing that affect you. Some of the problems that the current federal administration allows are quite obvious even in the Washington-D.C. You should visit the capital to observe most of the vehicles are made overseas and not in the USA. The foreign automakers should have people lobbying for them a lot since there are many of these cars within our nation's capital. These laws which the foreign car makers help pass are damaging our economy. These laws only help foreign companies and they pay little or no import duty on foreign items. How can this happen and why is congress protecting them more than their people who voted for them. The unemployment rate in Washington-DC is terrible. This city is the capital of our beautiful and great nation.

As the economy becomes more nettled at the local, state, and federal level, most of the politicians are slashing their salaries. Some have actually voted for an increase in salary. They slash away so it would affect the average American, the senior citizens, the needy, sick, and blind, and other handicapped people. The United States federal government takes billions of our tax dollars that you and I must give to the government to spend on other nations such as Afghanistan or Pakistan. We the people deserve the money, not other nations. It makes me mad to hear on the news that our government is giving away so much money. What about the Americans who must work a lot like me to survive? What about giving money to you since you work hard to live a better life? They are not giving us money so we must protest and ask for our government to only spend money on our soil to help the people become robust.

Our soldiers and Airmen are deployed on foreign land and they buy equipment made there. They should not do this but some don't know the consequences of their actions or they simply know but don't care how it affects the United States of America. The effect is significant and some slowly care to do anything about it. USA, why haven't you learned your lesson. We can send a man to the moon, but foreigners and Americans believe we can't make less complicated items such as LCD flat screens, Computers, and radios. We are not assembling any of these items so the taxpayers of the United States of America are robbed of their money when the military personnel, politicians, and other staff buy the foreign equipment when overseas or even in the United States of America.

Many of the foreign lands that our military is stationed at don't pay much to the expense of keeping our military troops to serve and protect that nation. They request our assistance with military power and also United States Dollars, albeit they don't want to help us. All they are doing is putting the American citizens out of work. They are slowly ending our hope as you read this book. The jobs that the United States of America has are slowly declining because of all the foreign jobs and labor. In many cities and states here in the United States of America, police officers are seen driving foreign motorcycles paid with your tax dollars, which lays off another American worker because that money doesn't circulate back in the American system.

Innocuous Americans are forced to acquire money any way they can to feed their family, and then the people will start killing other people. One can only imagine what will happen to our criminal justice system after all these people are arrested for murder. Will the criminal justice system be totally destroyed? Prisons are already overcrowded now and when many defendants are put in prisons, there will be so many that prisoners will need to be put on house arrest or the people in jail will be released so the death row inmates can be sent there. There are so many possibilities when the systems are overcrowded and so many criminals will be released from jail.

If foreign lands demand their money and we can't deliver, they will make a call and come again with their military to conquer our nation for the debt we owe to them. Once the foreigners arrive with their military, there will be a great war. We will find out who are not right from this situation but who are left after gunfire. There will be a huge war that will intimidate an abundance of people. Some of the Americans will surrender to the foreigners' military or even worse, they will fight for the inimical foreigners. We will not allow this to happen for we have too much pride. Our allies will be called from all around the world which will create a bigger war. Our allies will come to help us, and then China will call their allies to help them. This war is the destruction of man. This war will be an implacable war for many years. The war will be gloomy just like when an asteroid destroyed the dinosaurs many years ago. Please don't fear because we can change this occurrence. We can stop this from happening and now is the time to fix America.

Next, the maritime industry is what I want to talk about. You maritime people can go to different ports in the world and see how many American ships there are. How many American ship-yards still remain open? A lot of American shipyards are out of business. We have enough corporations going foreign and then they bring those same products back to the United States of America. The funny thing is that the Americans are buying these same products that put them out of a job. Unemployment will still rise every month with the help of the politicians who help the foreigners and give them more help than the American people. Some of these politicians are the traitors and they are not true Americans because if they were proud of their country and help their own people. I will write my words and these words have meaning. I speak the truth and I am concerned with our country.

Unfortunately, we have some traitors as our lawmakers and we need to make sure that we are meticulous when you vote. It's very difficult to see who the traitors are since they disguise themselves very well and they say they care for the American people but that is false. They only care for the money they make and not for the people. This is true because our economy is really bad and it will only get worse because of those same politicians who only know how to win elections. We built

highways with American tax dollars, now our enemy is utilizing those highways to drive foreign cars. Why can't we have more American cars on the roads? I drove today and observed so many foreign cars and not many American cars. If you don't believe what I am saying is true, then you should look for yourself. When you are in Wal-Mart or Best Buy look for at the products in the store and see where they are made. Most of them are not made in the United States of America. Why have we betrayed the nation where we have our allegiance? We need to restore America back to where she belongs. Stop buy foreign products and stop closing American plants because you will put yourself and your family out of a job.

CHAPTER 9 FINDING WORK

I n June 2009, the numbers of people who don't have work were at least 14,500,000 and this number was provided by the government. In the United States of America there are more people who don't have work than the government will reveal regardless of which political party is in power because the government likes to dissemble to mollify the people.

A question that many people ask is if they need a computer and internet access to find a job. One doesn't need to have a computer. There are ways to find a job without having a computer. You can always search in the newspaper in the job listing section and also one can walk or drive by the businesses and ask if they are hiring. I have done this years ago when I was a teenager and even when I first came to the University of South Florida. I walked by different departments to get a job and the first day when I have moved to the dorms at the University of South Florida I found a job. I asked, are you hiring? I found the job and it worked out well. You can also ask a friend to search online for you since he or she owns a computer. At least 74.7 percent of Americans use the Internet, which is around 227 million people who use a computer for personal or business reasons. You can actually just locate an internet café instead of asking a friend if you are in a rush. Some of the websites that you can use to find jobs are http://www.usajobs.gov, http://www.careerbuilder.com, or http://www.monster.com. Once you go to these sites, you must enter a search title of the job that you are looking for. One must realize that the employer usually hires people from within the company first since he or she already knows the business and the company knows what the employee can offer the company. The second person an employer wants to hire is someone who shows valid proof of their work. The last way that people can be hired is to use a curriculum vitae.

Remember, there is hope for everyone because people get promoted, people quit, employees die, and people are laid off or are terminated. With this said, there are always openings so never give up. Employers usually want to see that the person applying for the job has the following: Self-management skills, responsibility, experience, people skills, and talent. This is what the majority of any company wants to see someone have. Don't provide an interview that is insipid. These employers are inured to these qualities so make sure that you exemplify these qualities during the interview. Employers want to make sure that you know what you are doing or can learn quickly.

Make sure you do some research about the company so when you have an interview, you will know the products, services, and the history of the company. Employers also want to see compelling; loyalty, and persistence. Overall, they want to know what you can do that the other 32 candidates can't do which would benefit the company. There are many questions the employer can ask you and some of them are provided below. Make sure you study these questions so you can ingratiate yourself. You must not be inchoate at the interview because you will not obtain the position.

Random general questions for an interview:

What specific skills and qualities can you bring to our company?

Exemplify a time where you had to manage a stressful situation.

Where do you expect to be in 5 years?

What are your strengths and weaknesses? (The correct answer is that you are a perfectionist.)

Can you tell me about yourself? (To have a short statement will make you imperturbable so your answer is flawless)

Why have you left your last job? (Remain positive regardless of the reason. You should never say anything that would nettle the reputation of management, colleagues, or the organization.

Are you applying for other jobs (Be honest and don't spend a lot of time with the response)

What do you know about this organization?

Why do you want to work for this company?

What type of salary do you require? (Don't answer with a number. Say something like, that's a difficult question to answer.

Could you tell me the range for the position?

How long are you expecting to work with if we give you the job? (Tell them as long as you both feel that you are doing a great job)
Were you asked to leave a job? (Be honest and avoid negativity if you were asked to resign)

What is your philosophy at work? (Don't be garrulous; they just want a short and positive statement that benefits the company.)

How can you be an asset to the company? (Now is the time to be gregarious with your response. Explain your best qualities.)

Are you willing to relocate?

Describe your management style?

Describe your work ethic. (Emphasize beneficial qualities like determination.)

Do you have any questions for me? (Be prepared and have questions ready.)

Here are interview questions for an academic position:

Describe your research?

What people are you addressing and what books are popular, and how does your work relate with their work?

Do you have a publisher who is interested and what step are you with having you book or research published?

What is your philosophical style of teaching?

How will you inculcate?

What courses do you want to teach if you had your druthers and what books would you use? (some committees want to know what books you will utilize for teaching purposes)

Do you research to see what the department needs help with?

Explain how the students can value what you would teach them.

How has the research you done influenced your teaching methods?

How has your research helped your with teaching at an undergraduate level?

The university has an enrollment of hundreds of students for the course you are teaching. How would you manage the course and the students?

You can use power point slides and online assignments to reach all the students. This is a university where publications are critical when candidates for tenure are reviewed. Why will you get tenure over other candidates?

You should have a paper ready that exemplifies a subject different from your doctoral or thesis research.

Why do you want to teach at this college or university?

How can you contribute to the department?

Are you connected with other instructors, researchers, or professors?

What are the reactions of your spouse when you say that you have a job in another state?

This chapter should help you significantly when you look for a job. Remember, you must be unique and confident for the position. There are resources out there and I will update this book in the future when needed so I can help my people of the United States of America.

CHAPTER 10
BLACK-AMERICAN
ORGANIZATIONS

This is a letter to the black organizations here in the United States of America. These black organizations include PUSH, NAACP, and SCLC. All the members of these organizations must understand that here in the United States, the economy is not getting better anytime soon and the black-American population is becoming nettled the hardest. The crime rate and the unemployment rates are at their acme and these rates will continue to rise and Americans are living in an unaware society because the rates are not abating. As of November 5, 2010 the unemployment for the Black-American population was 16.3 percent. Everyone is feeling the burden and Rev. Jesse Jackson marched in Detroit for jobs and the United Nations is investigating whether consistent lack of employment is a human rights violation.

The only future you can count on will be from the black youth generation. They are our future without them; you will not have a future. Stop doing what you are doing and think about what went wrong and how you can save your beautiful country of America.

These black youth are unemployed and a significant portion of black adults are unemployed. I hope you are not naïve enough to believe it is the fault of the United States Government. If you taught your children right and wrong, each child would recognize who the United States Government is and they would know it is by the people and for the people of the United States of America. Do not blame the United States Government because you are blaming yourself.

What do you think is the paramount reason for the majority of unemployment in the United States of America? It is easy enough that some children will know. When American people buy foreign items, we don't need factories here in America. That is the sole problem and we should solve the problem. The market will always be here in the United States of America and when the factories return to America, you will have jobs and a great future. Explain to your family, friends, neighbors, and colleagues the sole problem and tell them to buy only American made products. You must be able to earn a great salary here in the United States of America and enjoy life.

There is no good life in welfare or unemployment line and if you don't soon, you will not have that to help you and your family. Please trust in God always because when you believe in God, you have a better relationship with your lover, family, and friends. When you step outside and look on the streets, you will find a plethora of foreign automobiles. Go to the supermarket or other stores and you will see that the majority of the items are made in foreign lands. Why do you buy these products? Is it because they are cheaper? I hope you understand that when you buy these foreign products, the money doesn't remain in the United States of America. The money is sent back to the foreign land which makes their economy stronger than ours. This must not happen. The United States of America must be over everything. Be proud of your nation and be proud of your flag so stop buying foreign products. When you buy these cars, you put yourself and other Americans out of work. Maybe the best thing for you to do is move to another nation, get a job and buy their items then we don't need to support you when you drive a foreign made car and wearing foreign clothes to the welfare and the unemployment line.

These foreign companies don't make cheaper and better items than us. Some of these governments pay for the majority of the costs when importing these products here and that is the reason you think they are cheaper to make. You will not collect unemployment for very long because there will be nothing going into the system. Some of these foreign people who manufacture these products don't contribute to the American system such as federal or state income taxes that you want to collect from. How can you buy this product? I just told you the consequences of buying foreign made products. Do not blame the United States Government or the foreign companies who market these products. You can only blame yourself for buying the foreign items. You must only blame yourself contrary to what people say now that you are unemployed and your children can't find a job. You will have plenty of time to take a break from your life and fathom what had happened in the United States of America.

Black-Americans are not the only people who are easily deceived. There are many races here in the United States of America who are deceived also because the unemployment rate is very high for all people. Just look around you and you will observe an abundance of Americans wearing foreign clothes and watching foreign Televisions and they know what time it is when they look at their foreign smart phones or watches. Just listen to what I have exemplified and inform the people of the consequences of their actions and what they can do to solve the problem. This must be the priority of the United States of American. My initiative is to restore power to the United States of America and restore jobs in our homeland.

We deserve this and we must take what is ours and we must challenge authority to help the initiative. My initiative is clear and please help me help you. Our strength is only as strong as the weakest link so let's create a robust chain which can't be broken. I want jobs for everyone at all levels of intelligence. Foreigners who are in our great land must know that they should become a citizen if they wish to prosper with us. We must give them an opportunity so they can exemplify their allegiance to our great nation. We should welcome them so they can contribute to the system and amalgamate our strength. Don't give up on the United States of America, because the United States of America has not given up on you.

CHAPTER 11 SCHOOLS AND STUDENTS

I had realized that most of these children in Primary and middle school don't understand the vicissitudes in the world because they are young and their brain is not developed. They only know how to play and I want to know what is in their future because they are the future of our beautiful nation. I hope they have a prosperous future here in the United States of America but that will be difficult with all the foreign cars I see on the road.

Toyota is a popular foreign car and that's because it is fuel efficient more than most cars. Why doesn't our government make laws which say that our car manufacturers must provide very fuel efficient cars? For this reason, there are many foreign cars bought by the American people. As I pass by schools during my errands or just to eat lunch with a friend, I watch so many foreign cars on the streets. It is terrible to see more foreign cars than American cars on the streets and we should be ashamed. These children grow up and look for jobs and most want a new car that is fuel efficient so they buy a foreign car. This is terrible and we need to stop this. These teenagers are graduating and they hope to find a job after high school while going to college but it doesn't work out like that. These jobs are already secured by others so these students remain unemployed. These students who don't have jobs will enroll in college and pursue their Bachelor degree and if they are smart enough, they will work continuously until they obtain a graduate degree. There are a plethora of people going to college at the moment because there are no jobs for unskilled laborers. These people go to college to pursue a specialized degree but they can't find a career after because there are many other college graduates who applied to the same job as you had.

Because there are so many going to school, the schools can charge more in tuition which would help them when building more structures however most of these students receive pell grants and student loans to pay for school because they can't find jobs or their family has been unemployed. It is detrimental for students to pay more money and some student can't afford the tuition increase but will need to find a way to do that. In Florida there was recently a 15 percent tuition and fee increase. Eight percent of this tuition increase is for general revenue approved from the Florida Board of Governors and the other seven percent is approved by the universities.

You should not be appalled by the tuition increase because you are still buying foreign products. The allocation from the state and the students' tuition rate is what the universities look at when deciding the budget so make sure you go out there and spend money on the lottery because that is the only way education will remain robust because in the state of Florida, the money from ticket sales assists with providing educational funds. Florida is not the only state that is implementing a tuition increase.

California State University students are preparing also because the fees will be increased to 15.5 percent by the next fall. The university had received the same amount of money as it had for the prior five years although they have 25,000 more students. The university officials reported that they must raise the student fees because of the budget cuts and the lack of state funding. There have been fewer course offerings and enrollment reductions.

Oklahoma all 25 public colleges asked for tuition and fee increases which totaled around 5.1 percent for residents and 4.8

percent for out of state residents in the year 2010. State colleges are seeing more enrollments and looming budget cuts from the state of Oklahoma during the upcoming fiscal year and making out with a year without increasing tuition or fees. The 5.1 percent tuition average increase for students who are residents at public colleges represent an average $6.14 increase per credit hour. Also the average increase for out of state residents is lower the 4.8 percent increase is actually a higher dollar amount. The dollar amount is $14.09 per credit hour of $307.80 for the next year. The tuition rates had increased and it is difficult currently for college graduates to find a job because there are so many people searching for the same job. If you continue to buy foreign products and you will see our economy abates further. Unfortunately the taxes will continue to rise because of the money is being sent to foreign lands because you buy foreign products. The tuition will not decrease until you buy more American products.

The national Education Association in June 2010 said that there are around 26,000 teachers who are in the depths of being unemployed in the state of California, about 20,000 in Illinois, 8,000 in Michigan, 6,000 in New Jersey, and 13,000 in New York. Next, states with dwindling tax revenues are made to annihilate the basic public services and school budgets are nettled with these significant cuts. This makes unions, teachers, staff professors, and students in the United States of America demanding that the government at the state and federal level provide emergency funding in order to prevent theannihilation of thousands of instructor related jobs and school personnel. The secretary of education wants to keep more than 300,000 teacher jobs by asking Congress to appropriate $23 billion in emergency money funds.

United States employers are expected to hire 7 percent fewer college graduates from this year's class of 2010 versus last year. For those young students who are under the age of 26, they can remain on their parents' health insurance plan and freelance or be a bartender all the way through the recession without having many worries.

The tuition rates had increased and it is difficult currently for college graduates to find a job because there are so many people searching for the same job. If you continue to buy foreign products and you will see our economy abates further. Unfortunately the taxes will continue to rise because of the money is being sent to foreign lands because you buy foreign products. The tuition will not decrease until you buy more American products. Next, are the main reasons why college graduates can't find a job.

1. Lack of interpersonal skills

Most people think that one just needs skills and the knowledge for that specific job, however that statement is incorrect. The majority of employers want to see social skills in the prospective employees because communication is everything. Will you fit in well with the staff? Can you adapt to different personalities? Some companies have a person who has a different personality than the other co- worker beside you. One should be able to adapt to the vicissitudes and people who you will work with. Are you a positive person? Are you easy to get along with? These are some of the questions you must think about before applying to the company because if you have some bad habits, then you must change the bad habits. My family has interviewed people for jobs before and they would talk about that specific person after she left the building. They wanted to know if the majority had liked her based on her social skills and likeability rather than her skills. Make sure you are nice to everyone when going to an interview because they will talk about you after you leave.

2. Accumulable competition

We are in a new era where everyone has the opportunity to study in college. Numerous college applications have been sent so they could possibly obtain a great job but with the plethora of college students, they must have something more than a degree to make them qualified candidates.

3. No follow up contact

You sent a cover letter and curriculum vitae, however heard nothing from the prospective employer. Do not be intimidated because the employer wants to see that you are persistent and determined to obtain that position. Be dauntless and call the employer back, send an email, or send a letter in the mail. This simple technique will sequester you from the others who do not follow up. Take the initiative and contact them because it can only help you.

4. No preparation on the curriculum vitae and cover letter

The purpose of the curriculum vitae and cover letter presentation is to be invited to the interview of a potential employer. Your cover letter and curriculum vitae is the first impression so make it tantalizing. You should send a paper curriculum vitae and also an email with your curriculum vitae. When you send the paper versions, please make them appealing to the eyes. By doing this, the employer will need to observe it by their hands and eyes. If it pleases them by holding the curriculum vitae and cover letter by reading them, then you have proceeded to the next step. One must understand that the curriculum vitae could manifest how easily someone becomes depressed by abating their self-esteem.

The reason for depression is that the job hunting strategy was a failure, however please don't be discouraged. It is understood that the detriment of the feeling one exemplifies is from the curriculum vitae. An abundance of people will believe something is wrong with them because they had used this technique many times which resulted in no interviews. Some students searching for careers never develop an entire stable mind again and therefore the curriculum vitae should be labeled as followed: Caution, this content may be hazardous to your mental health. Some college students will stop searching for a job prematurely because of their mental health is unstable.

Some experts recommend sending a cover letter instead of the class curriculum vitae which summarizes everything you have accomplished. Google is a great and neutral friend to everyone so if you don't know how to create a curriculum vitae or a cover letter, just search with Google. You should also consider having a career portfolio because

this will exemplify all the qualities and accomplishments you possess. I spoke with my brother Brandon Frohne about his success with being a Director so I asked him how he had accomplished everything in a minuscule amount of time. He told me that created a career portfolio which had everything that an employer wants to know when deciding the fate of that potential employee. If they didn't like the way it felt in their hands and eyes, they will discard your request for an interview. You just can't win them over with your smile. Your writing will exemplify what you know and this will do most of the talking for you. Make sure you take the time to have a great presentation. Most people say that presentation is everything and those people are correct. When you describe yourself in your curriculum vitae and cover letter, don't be coy. Describe yourself with true action words. There is a significant difference when you use these words. If you don't utilize these words you will deplore your chance to find work. You should also find a professional editor or you can edit it and use longer words that people don't use often. You should use some of the words that you study from the GRE vocabulary.

Remember this entire process must not be dilapidated so invest a minuscule amount of time to produce a professional curriculum vitae and cover letter so that you can earn a lot of money.

5. Be dexterous with interview questions

You have made it past the curriculum vitae step and now it is time for the interview. Never digress when they ask you questions. They will ask many questions so do your research on the company that is interviewing you. They will ask you sample questions like this:

What are you strengths and what are your weaknesses?
Why should we hire you?
Why do you want to work for our company? Exemplify a time where you had to be a leader to solve a problem?

Tell me about yourself?
There are a plethora of online sources to help you prepare for this interview. Prepare and try to remember all the answers and questions for the interview. Prepare for the interview as such:

Give examples of what is written on your curriculum vitae and cover letter. Have extra copies of your curriculum vitae, research papers, or publications that you had made to give to the interviewers at the time of the interview.

Ask them questions when they give you permission such as:

What is your management style?
Who will be my boss?
What type of work will I be doing? Can I take a tour of the company?
Ask about the benefits package
What type of advancement is possible?

6. No unique qualities

You must be different however only in a positive way so they will see this as an advantage for their company. You are the sole person who knows why and how you are different than the other applicants so make it happen. If you don't have this unique style; the company will ponder you are just an average person and they can find average people anywhere.

7. A minuscule amount of work experience or none:

An abundance of college students continuously assume that their prestigious degree will make them qualified for the position so a plethora of college students party while in college and are not actively engaged in extracurricular activities. Their work experience is dilapidated and they don't want to pursue hands on training while they are still studying and this is detrimental to themselves because employers want to have someone yoke with them so they can amalgamate as one company with experience. A plethora of corporations desire work experience from candidate and will not hire unless you have work experience. You should work internships while in school because I company would like to keep the same intern who worked for them since they have the skills and know the work ethics from that person. It is beneficial for both the student and the company to work an internship.

8. Networking deficiency

Statistics exemplify that numerous people obtain positions through referrals. When a corporation has trust in an employee, the corporation will rely on the person who the employee has referred. The trustworthy networking strategy exemplifies the efficacy of the employee to his company. Make connections with friends so that you could possibly obtain a position this way.

Because a robust curriculum vitae is vital to everyone I will exemplify what is needed to create a tantalizing and beneficial curriculum vitae. The curriculum vitae amalgamates your past and present experiences and a document is needed to exemplify your credentials. Your curriculum vitae should contain the following:

Education
-scholarships, assistantships, or fellowships -extracurricular activities or organizations -awards for your studies
-school committees
-university publications
-self published books or other publications

Publications, seminars, or research projects
-Include papers, articles, chapters, or books that you have published
-Make sure to include ISBN or Kindle number and include when

the publication was made

-Presentations in seminars where you gave lectures or contributed
-Provide topics and subjects which you contributed

Volunteer work
-Include churches, schools, synagogues, non-profit organizations, or other religious organizations

Logistics, conference management, or events
-Include the budget you had and how many people - -who worked for you and how many people attended the events.

Computer work
-Software: Include software that you have created or software that you have utilized which helped the company
-Hardware: Include hardware that you developed. -Websites: Include websites that you have created and how they have affected you or companies in a positive way

Small companies create many jobs however most of those jobs are on foreign land. Fortunately, there are still a few jobs which remain in the United States of America. One doesn't need to worry about finding the boss because in a small company the boss is usually easy to contact. These jobs are easier to obtain because you don't need to continuously wait until there is a position available. In a small company there is no human resources to eliminate you based on credentials. A great quality of a small business is that most are growing therefore resulting in a new position that you could possible get but you need to assure them that they need you more than the other candidates.

You already understand that finding someone to interview you is an arduous task. Because humans are voluble, this means everyone has friends including the person who has the power to hire someone. After you find the person who has the power to hire, then this will solve the prayer from the corporation and also from the potential employee. Find out what the corporation needs to make them grow and then put yourself into this equation. If you can't find out what their need is then don't worry, because that will be revealed later. The person will be appalled because you have found out who he or she is without a meeting. College students, this interview is for you and it will be like a first date. You and the employer you want to work with will talk to decide if you are good enough to be with them. In the next passage, there will be bad qualities the company will worry about:

-Don't bring bad energy into the company
-You exemplify a minuscule amount of work ethic -You will be a burden on them and cost them a lot of money
-You will not commit an entire day of work continuously
-You will not cope well with other co-workers or will have a demeanor which the boss doesn't like. -You will remain on the job for a short period of time and quit without notice.
-You will be told what to do and not think for yourself.
-You will demonstrate bad habits such as dishonesty or a credibility deficiency
-You will be absent too much

To all college students, remain talking half the time and listen half the time while in the interview. This is very important and the employer is searching for this balance. If you overwhelm the interviewers during the interview, they will think that you will ignore protocol and not benefit the company. College students can consider these things when they want to become hired.

Bad habits which you should not have during the interview -The employer will search to see if you smoke tobacco. The candidate who doesn't smoke will have a greater chance to be employed than the smoker.

-The employer doesn't like when you degrade or your prior employers
-Not thanking the interview committee for the interview. You should shake hands with everyone in the room. Send a thank you email to the interview committee since this exemplifies yourself

as a determined person who has business etiquette. Not many college students send a thank you letter or email and this should be done after every interview.

Negative values
-Don't have an excessive tardy record
-Don't exemplify laziness tendencies and don't have a motivation deficiency
-Don't be arrogant and don't be very aggressive

-Don't complain about prior employers and don't complain about the day or drive to the interview -Don't exemplify a credibility deficiency during the conversation about your past, present, or future

Appearance and presentation

For males

-Don't have bad breath during your interview -Don't have a smell of tobacco, drugs, alcohol on your person
-Don't have a dirty appearance, therefore you must take a bath or shower before the interview
-Don't wear dirty clothes so take the time to clean them before the interview
-Polish your black shoes before the interview -Don't have lazy posture
-Don't have dirty teeth so brush them, floss, and use mouthwash

For females

-Don't have excessive makeup on your face -Don't have dirty fingernails
-Don't have long fingernails
-Don't have bad breath or smell of alcohol, drugs, or tobacco

-Don't wear perfume
-Wear something professional such as a business suit

Self-confidence deficiency

-Don't interrupt continuously during the interview -Don't provide hesitant responses
-Don't give one word responses because it shows an intelligence deficiency
-Don't speak very softly albeit you are in a small interview room
-Don't speak very loud so that your voice is heard in other rooms
-Don't exaggerate your abilities or achievements

Each expert will say that you should send a thank you note or email to the person or committee who conducted the interview. Sending these thank you emails makes your appearance professional and many don't send thank your emails to these potential employers. The interview committee will also recognize that you are a friendly person and demonstrate great customer service skills. When you send a thank you email it helps the interview committee remember you and this will be helpful when they are asked what they think of the candidate. The thank you email will also give you time to add anything which you had forgot while in the interview. Remember to make this thank you email brief and if you don't have access to a computer with internet, you can go to the public library or your university library. Try to refrain from using a lot of paper since trees provide us oxygen to live therefore I ask you to send emails rather than a thank you letter via USPS or FedEx.

Friends and college students, I understand your frustrations because I am a college student myself.

College Students and their salary negotiation skills

This is a sensitive subject and most don't negotiate a salary. Negotiating a salary is important and you should always question the salary and negotiate before accepting the new position. Most people are intimidated to ask and negotiate for the fear that they will not be hired with that employer. I have written some topic which will help you:

I. Obtaining the most money an employer will pay

The goal of the employer is to save every penny they can and your priority is to bring home a high salary for the job description you will do.

II. Research the conventional salaries for your concentrated area of work and for that employer

One can negotiate a salary and this is done with courage and patience. You must have courage because the open starting number is most likely the lowest salary they will offer and it is your time to make say you want another number since you have done your research and you can possibly get $10,000 more than what you have currently just because you researched the salaries for this job and for the company. There is a significant penalty when you don't research the salaries because you will receive a low salary. Once you access the internet you can go to different websites to find the salaries. Google is a great neutral friend that will help you on your quest so invest 8 hours of salary research and you will see that it will benefit you after you are hired. Type the salary for your job at the employer and that should be everything you need to find the salary range they offer.

When you can't find the salary range then you can go to the Bureau of Labor Statistics online and find general salaries for your concentration. The next way to find out what type of salary range you can expect is to go to the public or university library. You can ask librarians how to find the salary range for your concentration. You might not need to do a salary search if you apply to an entry level position like at a restaurant. If you are going to work as a carpenter for a general contractor, ask around town to find out what type of salary or hourly wage they pay. After you find out what the competitor pays, then you can reference this when you apply to the company you want to work with.

III. Don't be the first to initiate the salary range

You want the employer to be the first to say anything pertaining to a salary because if you are the first to mention it, you will probably lose the negotiation of the salary. You must indirectly force the employer to pay the most salary although they only want to pay the least amount possible. An experienced employer knows how the salary game work so they will make sure that you speak about the salary first. If they are inexperienced then you should make a tantalizing request. If they are experienced they will ask you, what type of salary do you want? This is not a benevolent gesture because they want you to be the first to say a number. Don't say a number and you should give this rebuttal or a rebuttal similar. Tell them, you had made this position so you have a number in mind and I am interested to know what that number is. This will confuse them and it should force them to give you a number then you can request for a higher salary.

IV. Close the deal on the salary negotiation

Ask the interviewer about what benefits are involved such as health insurance, dental insurance, vacation, retirement plans, and life insurance. Negotiate which plans interest you and then formulate a hypothesis what the salary range the employer is offering. You should make your own salary range based on what you think the employer will offer. Hypothetically speaking, the employer will offer between $33,000 and $43,000 as a salary. You will start your range with the least amount you will accept. This number should be less than the highest they will offer and your highest number should be proportional to what you have done based on salary research. After the employer gives you a number then you should rebuttal with this statement. I understand that the economy abates, however I think my productivity and abilities will justify between $40,000 and $50,000 salary. Be prepared to give a demonstration or presentation why your own salary range will justify their salary range. They will want to know how you can benefit the company and save them money. They want to know how they can be more lucrative as a company too. If the company can't afford to hire you with the salary range you have requested, inform them that you will consider offering them a portion of your time at the salary they say they can afford.

You can work a couple days out of the week and your productivity will be high. Request an employee contract or agreement letter saying what the benefits they will give you and the salary range. The interviewing committee could forget or deny later what they have told you and this document is proof of the agreement.

CHAPTER 12
AMERICAN SENIOR CITIZENS AND FOREIGNERS

You outstanding people are the people of the past in the United States of America, and your children are the current and your grand-children will be the future of the United States of American and the world. The vicissitudes today in the United States of America didn't arrive by chance. The vicissitudes are here because we manifested them. The United States of America have slowly nettled themselves for years because American factories have gone out of business and shipped the once American factories over to a foreign land. While those manufacturing jobs are on foreign soil, they will never contribute to the social security administration here in the United States of America. Because they don't contribute you will not collect social security for a lengthy time.

I don't understand what cause you to react this way in the past. It's a possibility that you never thought about the future and therefore the United States of America economy became dilapidated because of your thought deficiency. I see more problems occur in the United States because of the American people don't have jobs. The national debt is approximately 22 trillion dollars as of April 16, 2019 and we have a population 309 million people so this means that each person has a debt they owe to the government of $44,440. This nation will be in a financial collapse soon so precautionary measures must be enforced. Soon you will not have a medicare program and which is vital to all senior citizens because of detrimental vicissitudes. It is uncanny how you and your grand children still continuously buy foreign made products because we might not have a robust nation in the future. You must have not taught your children and grand children the rules of the market because the same mistakes are continuously made which happened in the past.

The only way to see a bright future is to stop buying foreign products made in foreign lands. After you start buying American products, you should have pride because this will enable your children and grand children to have prosperous lives and high paying salaries. Then you can apologize to your family for making detrimental decisions in the past and look forward to a bright horizon and a proud flag of the United States of America. Make sure teach your children and grand-children not to make the same errors you have made when they become senior citizens. To all senior citizens, you know that the majority look up to you for guidance since you have more experience and wisdom than the younger population so educate the people and tell them to buy products only made in the United States of America. The United States was founded on ending foreign dependence and we need to continuously exemplify that we are independent and we will continue to accumulate our strength.

You senior citizens have lived through the gloomy times and you know it becomes better with teamwork. The teamwork is demonstrated by aliens, refugees, and American citizens.

If you are a foreigner and wish to make money from the United

States of America, I invite you to visit our nation and slowly show our people which is our government that your allegiance is within the United States of America. We will not scold you for denouncing your citizenship with your native country. We will invite you so that you can live a happier and more lucrative life with your family here in the United States of America. You will pay taxes like other American citizens and be united with us no matter your religion or ethnicity. Senior citizens, you understand unity more than us since you have more wisdom than younger people.

We wish to unite all with opportunities that exist and opportunities that must be invented. The first step to show your allegiance was buying this book now it's your time to tell the people what you have learned from me. Our nation is beautiful and we must continuously amalgamate ideas, jobs, and people so that we can be the nation who can offer jobs to everyone who seeks them.

www.ingramcontent.com/pod-product-compliance
Lightning Source LLC
Chambersburg PA
CBHW062110280526
45788CB00003B/1422